The Mystery and Magnificence of Mary

Carlo Maratta, *Nativita*, 1655, Staatliche Kunstsammlungen, Dresden

The Mystery and Magnificence of Mary

in Paintings & Poems

Neill Reilly

SteinerBooks ≈ 2025

Front cover: Sandro Botticelli, *The Virgin and Child* (*The Madonna of the Book*), 1480–81 (detail)
Museo Poldi Pezzoli, Milan

Back cover: Raphael, *Madonna della seggiola* (*Madonna of the Chair*), 1513–14,
Palazzo Pitti, Florence

LIBRARY OF CONGRESS CONTROL NUMBER: 2025947190
ISBN: 978-1-62148-406-6

Printed in the United States of America by Integrated Books International

Contents

"Omnia ad Jesum per Mariam"

All to Jesus through Mary

Preface

This book celebrates the spiritual mysteries and magnificence of Mary and her mission. She has inspired humanity for more than two thousand years and will continue to do so long into the future.

Over several weeks, I received a series of poems that focus on Mary and reflect some of the mysteries surrounding her life on earth. A few months later, the idea evolved to use these poems as introductions to each of the mysteries with great works of art.

The selected artworks portray pivotal moments in Mary's life, from Immaculate Conception and Annunciation to more recent apparitions of her being and The Last Judgment. The artists' works represent epiphanies that invite us to behold and partake inwardly in each mystery.

> These great artists seem to have been present
> in the moment they are depicting.
> If we use our imagination,
> these pictures are alive.
> We can create an internal, living tableau.
> The tableau is not a copy of the art.
> It is our own creation.
> We can enter into them
> and abide in the experience.
> We also can become present in that moment.
> Beholding art becomes a perception.
> A perception of the eternal that resides in each of us.

Giotto di Bondone, *Joachim and Anne* [Mary's parents] *Meeting at the Golden Gate*, 1305, Scrovegni Chapel, Padua, Veneto, Italy

1 *Immaculate Conception*

What a mystery!

Mysteries are to be beheld.

They often do not make logical sense.

That does not negate their reality.

The word *mystery* has its Greek root in *Myste*—

one who has been initiated into sacred rites.

Mary had an Immaculate Conception.

She was conceived without sin, immaculate.

Therefore, she could be the vessel for Christ.

We should all strive to be immaculate, unstained,

to create our own vessel to receive the Christ within.

Diego Velázquez, *The Immaculate Conception*, 1618–19, The National Gallery, London

Giovanni Battista Tiepolo, *The Immaculate Conception*, 1767–68, Museo del Prado, Madrid

2. *Annunciation*

"How can this be?" Luke 1:26

What a stunning question for a thirteen-year-old girl

to ask an Archangel.

Gabriel's classic answer to Mary's question sums up all creation.

"For with God nothing shall be impossible." Luke 1:37

How could anyone that young be so strong

as to question an Archangel

and then say Yes to God

to the most important event in all time?

Jesus later restated Gabriel's exact truth.

"With man this is impossible,

but with God all things are possible." Matt 19:26

Fra Angelico, *La Anunciación,* ca. 1426, Museo del Prado, Madrid

Robert Campin, *Mérode Altarpiece: Annunciation Triptych*, 1427–32, The Cloisters, New York City

Sandro Botticelli, *Cestello Annunciation*, 1489, Uffizi, Florence

Anonymous, plate from *An Illustrated History of the Lord of Heaven Who Became Incarnate in the Flesh*, 1637, Jinjiang Church, Fujian Province, China

Henry Ossawa Tanner, *The Annunciation*, 1898, Philadelphia Museum of Art

Andrea della Robbia, *Annunciation*, 1475, Assumption of Mary Basilica, La Verna, Italy

John William Waterhouse, *Annunciation*, 1914, private collection

3. The Visitation

How brave can a thirteen-year-old girl be?

How courageous to say Yes.

How kind to visit Elizabeth, her pregnant cousin.

How determined to find out if the Angel is correct about Elizabeth?

Can the older woman bear a child?

Upon hearing Mary's voice,

John, the child in Elizabeth's womb, leapt for joy.

John is the first to bear witness to Christ.

Elizabeth and Mary praise God.

Mary sings *The Magnificat.*

"And Mary remained with her for about three months and then returned to her home." (Luke 1:39–56)
Carl Bloch, *The Visitation*, 1866, Frederiksborg Castle, Hillerød, Denmark

The Visitation, 12th-century fresco, St. George Church, Kurbinovo, North Macedonia

Jacques Daret, *Visitation*, ca. 1435, from *St. Vaast Altarpiece of the Virgin*, Staatliche Museen, Berlin

Pontormo, *Carmignano Visitation* (Mary and Elizabeth with handmaids), 1528, Rectory of Saints Michael and Francis, Carmignano, Italy

Robert Anning Bell, *Mary in the House of Elizabeth*, 1917, Tate Britain, London

4. *Nativity*

"The Logos became flesh and dwelt among us." John 1:14

What if Mary had said No to the Incarnation?

What if the nine-month-pregnant Mary

    had said No to travel from Nazareth to Bethlehem?

What if, after giving birth to Jesus,

    she had said No to fleeing to Egypt?

Mary is eternally Yes.

In all times and places Mary says Yes to God

    and to us.

Fra Angelico, *The Nativity*, 1440, Basilica di San Marco, Florence

Sandro Botticelli, *The Mystical Nativity*, 1500–01, National Gallery, London

Domenico Ghirlandaio, *Adoration of the Shepherds*, 1483–85, Santa Trinita, Florence

Fra Angelico & Fra Filippo Lippi, *Adoration of the Magi*, ca. 1450, National Gallery of Art, Washington, D.C.

Gerard van Honthorst, *Adoration of the Shepherds*, 1622, Pomeranian State Museum, Greifswald, Germany

William-Adolphe Bouguereau *The Madonna of the Roses*, 1903, Lyndhurst, Tarrytown, New York

Andrea della Robbia, *Madonna and Child with Three Cherubs*, 1475 until 1500, Louvre, Paris

Raphael, The Sistine Madonna, 1513–14, Gemäldegalerie Alte Meister, Dresden

Albrecht Dürer, *Mary among a Multitude of Animals*, ca. 1503, The Albertina, Vienna

Anonymous, *Virgin of Pomata with St. Nicholas Tolentino and St. Rose of Lima*, ca. 1750, Brooklyn Museum, Brooklyn

5. *The Wedding Feast at Cana*

What better moment for the first manifestation of His Glory?
A wedding celebrating the love of two individuals for one another.
Mary, ever kind, notices the host is running out of wine.
She implores her son to help.
Somewhat reluctantly, but ever dutiful,
He grants His mother's request.
By turning water into wine, the wedding feast may continue.
A loving act that is so practical
and foreshadows the Transubstantiation at The Last Supper.
Mary's sage advice resounds through the ages.
"Whatsoever he saith unto you, do it." John 2:5

Lavinia Fontana, *The Wedding Feast at Cana*, ca. 1580, J. Paul Getty Museum, Los Angeles

Jesus orders six jars to be filled with water during the wedding meal at Cana; Gérard David, *Les noces de Cana, avec Jean de Sedano, son fils et son épouse*, 16th century, Musée du Louvre, Paris

Xu Jihua, *Depiction of the Wedding at Cana and the Miracle of Jesus Turning Water into Wine*, 1934–37, Société des Auxiliaires des Missions Collection, Whitworth University, Spokane, WA

Maerten de Vos, *The Marriage at Cana,* 1596–97, Cathedral of Our Lady, Antwerp, Belgium

Tintoretto, The *Wedding Feast at Cana,* ca. 1545, Isabella Stewart Gardner Museum, Boston

6. *Lazarus*

"Jesus wept." John 11:35

Maybe raising Lazarus was the straw that broke the camel's back.

Christ performed a miracle in public that led to great unrest.

The Scribes, Pharisees, and Sadducees feared a revolt

would trigger Roman destruction of the Temple.

"Caiaphas, being the high priest that same year, said unto them,

'Ye know nothing at all,

nor consider that it is expedient for us, that one man should die for the people,

and that the whole nation perish not.'" John 11:49–51

James Tissot, *Jesus Wept*, 1886–96, Brooklyn Museum, New York

Henry Ossawa Tanner, *The Resurrection of Lazarus*, 1896, Musée d'Orsay, Paris

Rembrandt. *The Raising of Lazarus,* ca. 1632. Los Angeles County Museum of Art

Vincent van Gogh, *The Raising of Lazarus after Rembrandt*, 1890, Van Gogh Museum, Amsterdam

7. The Passion

How can a mother watch her child be whipped,
then scorned, spat upon and reviled by an entire city?
Walk with Him to his cruel death?
How can Mary have said Yes to all of the Passion?

Théodore Chassériau, *Christ in the Garden of Olives*, 1840, Musée des Beaux-Arts de Lyon, France

Bartolomeo di Tommaso, *The Betrayal of Christ*, 1445–50, Metropolitan Museum of Art, New York

James Tissot, *The Kiss of Judas*, 1886–94, The Brooklyn Museum, NY

Antonio Ciseri, *Ecce Homo* (Behold the man), 1871–91, Gallery of Modern Art, Palazzo Pitti, Florence

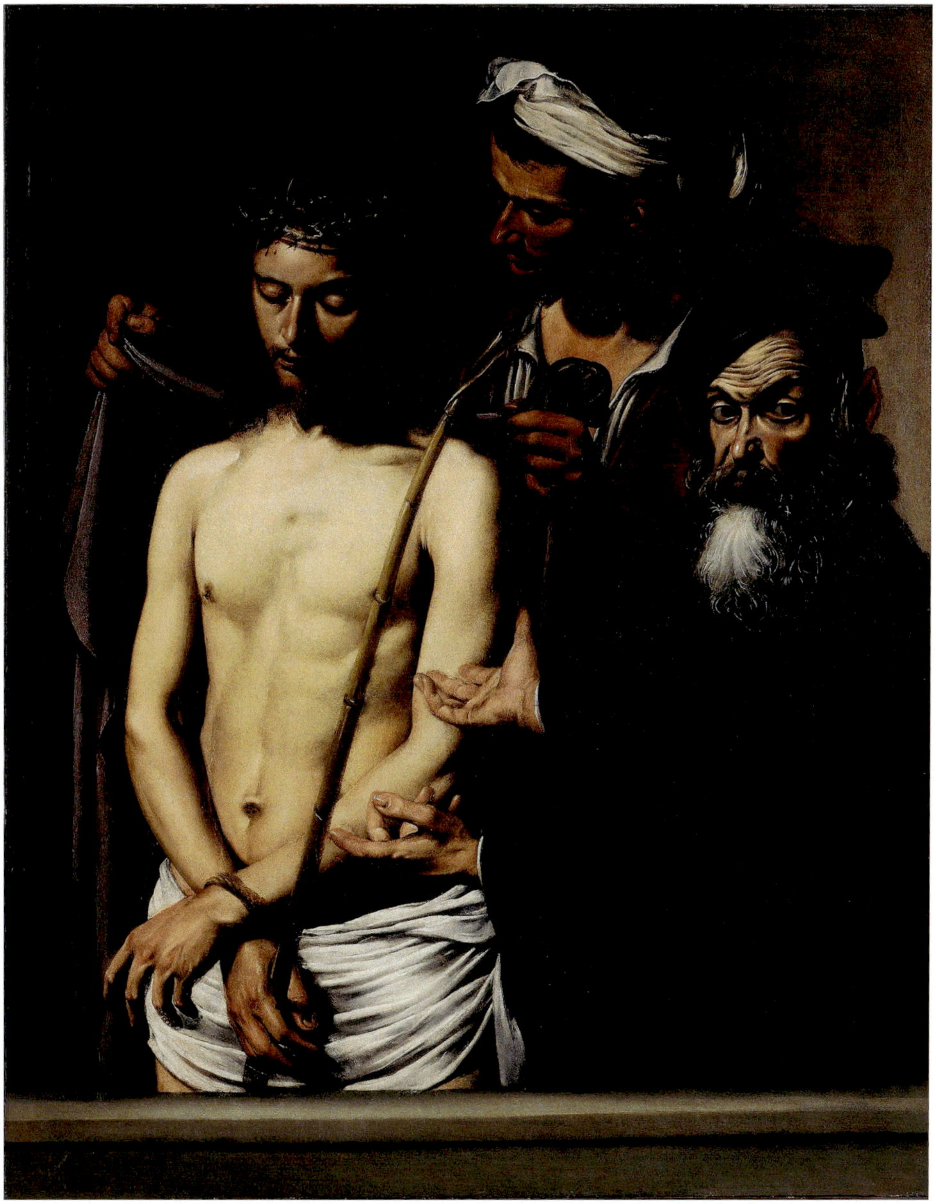

Caravaggio, *Ecce Homo*, 1605, Palazzo Bianco, Genoa, Italy

Fra Angelico, *The Mocking of Christ* (detail), 1440–42 Convent of San Marco, Florence

Vincent de Beauvais, *The Mocking of Christ* (*Speculum historiale*), ca. 1396, Bibliotheque nationale de France, Paris,

Albrecht Dürer, *The Flagellation*, 1509, The Metropolitan Museum of Art, New York

Raphael, *Christ Falling on the Way to Calvary*, 1514–16, Museo del Prado, Madrid

James Tissot, *Jesus Meets His Mother*, 1886-94, Brooklyn Museum, Brooklyn

Titian, *Christ Carrying the Cross*, 1565, Museo del Prado, Madrid

8. Crucifixion

The darkest moment in all time.
The fate of humanity in the balance.
Can Jesus endure all and not give into the temptation
to come down from the cross?
Mary, most courageous of all, stands by His side
with John, Mary Magdalen and the other Mary.
Christ's suffering is complete,
body, soul and spirit.
If He can pass the trial,
all will be saved.
For this horrendous moment He was born.
Mary never leaves His side.
Christ is tested to the core of His being.
By accepting death, He conquers Death
and sets humanity free.
The darkest moment becomes the most glorious moment,
The Turning Point in Time.

Fra Angelico, *The Crucifixion*, ca. 1420–23, Metropolitan Museum, New York

Jacopo Tintoretto, *Crucifixion*, 1565, Scuola Grande di San Rocco, Venice

Masaccio, *Holy Trinity*, 1426–28, Santa Maria Novella, Florence

James Tissot, *What Our Lord Saw from the Cross*, ca. 1886–94. Brooklyn Museum, New York

Fra Angelico, *Saint Dominic Adoring the Crucifixion* (detail), 1437–46, Museo San Marco, Florence

9. Descent from the Cross

Oh, what a ghastly site.

To see your beloved son's wrent body

  torn from life

  and passed along from cross to ground.

Naked as Adam and Eve,

  yet having saved us all from death and sin.

The Turning Point in Time.

Peter Paul Rubens, *The Descent from the Cross*, 1612–14, Cathedral of Our Lady, Antwerp

Rembrandt, *The Descent from the Cross*, 1633, Alte Pinakothek, Kunstareal, Germany

Rogier van der Weyden, *Descent from the Cross*, 1435–40, detail,
Mary Salomas (Mary's half sister), Museo del Prado, Madrid

10. *Pietà*

Sing in me, O muse, of the glories of Mary!
Bravest of all women.
Nay of all humans.
Who held her beloved child in her arms as an infant
    and now as the crucified, innocent Holy One of God.
Mary's soul cried out again, this time in pain.
"How can this be?" Luke 1:34
What anguish.
What sorrow.
"Yea, a sword shall pierce through thy own soul also,
    that the thoughts of many hearts may be revealed." Luke 2:35
Mary said Yes to the Incarnation
    all the way to the Excarnation.
Mary said Yes to the sword piercing her very soul.
Bravest of all.
Her sacrificial love helped to fulfill God's covenant.
Mary, you are Blessed.
We are all blessed by your acts of love.
You reveal the thoughts of our hearts.
Immaculate Mary!

Michaelangelo, *Pietà (Madonna della Pietà)*, 1498–99, Saint Peter's Basilica, Vatican City

Caravaggio, *The Entombment of Christ*, 1603–04, Pinacoteca Vaticana, Vatican City

Rembrandt, *The Entombment of Christ*, 1633–35, Hunterian Art Gallery, University of Glasgow

Carl Heinrich Bloch, *Burial of Christ*, 1865–79,
Museum of National History, Frederiksborg Castle, Hillerød, Denmark

William Blake, *Christ in the Sepulchre, Guarded by Angels*, 1808, Victoria and Albert Museum, London

11. *Resurrection*

What glory!

What triumph!

Death and sin are conquered!

Did Mary behold the Resurrected Christ?

No proof that Mary saw Him.

No proof that she did not.

Silence on this subject cannot affirm it did not happen.

It is hard to imagine that He did not long to see her

 and rejoice with her

 and soothe her pierced soul.

Albrecht Dürer, *Christ Appearing to His Mother*, 1510–11, Metropolitan Museum of Art, New York

Hans Memling, *Resurrection of Christ*, 15th century, Budapest Museum of Fine Arts

James Tissot, *The Resurrection*, ca. 1890, Brooklyn Museum, New York

Fra Angelico, *Women at the Empty Tomb*, 1437–46, Museo di San Marco, Florence

Luca Giordano, *The Resurrection*, after 1665, Residenzgalerie, Salzburg, Austria

12. *Ascension*

How to comprehend?
Your crucified son, risen and rising
back to His Heavenly Father?

Giotto, *The Ascension*, 1303, Scrovegni Chapel, Padua, Italy

Benvenuto Tisi, *Ascension of Christ*, ca. 1515, Galleria Nazionale d'Arte Antica, Rome

Benjamin West, *The Ascension*, 1801, Denver Art Museum

13. *Pentecost*

At the Annunciation, the Holy Spirit overshadowed Mary.
The power of God became manifested in Mary and through Mary.
At Pentecost the Holy Spirit again overshadowed Mary
and all His disciples.
The Holy Spirit, the divine fire, cleansed all.
By following her Yes
they became like Mary, immaculate,
worthy vessels of the Lord.
Like Mary, they sang their own songs,
their own Magnificats.

Jean Restout the Younger, *Pentecost*, 1732, Louvre, Paris

Joseph Ignaz Mildorfer, *Pentecost*, 1750s, Hungarian National Museum, Budapest

Jan Joest, *Pentecost*, 1505–08, St. Nicholas Church, Kalkar, Germany

14. *The Assumption of Mary*

Rising Heavenward,
yet never leaving her children on earth.
All ways loving.
All ways connected.
Her love knows no bounds.
The Mother of all.
Her Yes resounds
throughout all eternity

Fra Angelico, *The Death and the Assumption of the Virgin* (detail), ca. 1432, Isabella Stewart Gardner Museum, Boston

Peter Paul Rubens, *The Assumption of the Virgin Mary*, ca. 1618, Museum Kunstpalast, Düsseldorf

Titian, *The Assumption of Mary*, 1516–1518, Santa Maria Gloriosa dei Frari, Venice

15. *The Book of Revelation*

What a vision!

What a beholding of Mary!

Her centrality in the battle between Christ and the devil.

Her battle and love never end.

She is eternally loyal to Christ.

Eternal mother of all.

Mary "bears all things, believes all things,

hopes all things, endures all things."

1 Corinthians 13:7

Francisco de Zurbarán, *Immaculate Conception*, 1630, Museo del Prado, Madrid
Some artists connect the Immaculate Conception with the Book of Revelation

16. *Apparitions*

Too numerous to count.

All subject to doubt.

Doubt becomes overcome.

Justice is done.

Mary's presence is known.

To the devout she is shown.

Often poor, uneducated and young.

They end up shining like the sun.

Maitrejean Louis, *The Apparition of Virgin Mary in Lourdes*,
engraving from "Religious teaching through the eyes. Wonderful Album," 1910

Juan Diego, *Our Lady of Guadalupe*, Basilica of Our Lady of Guadalupe (detail), 16th century, Mexico City

17. *The Second Coming*

Glory, glory, glory!

What bliss!

What joy!

What triumph!

"Abide in Me

As I abide in you." John 15:4

"I am with you always,

even unto the end of the world." Matt 28:20

Anonymous, Icon: *The Second Coming*, 18th century, Sotheby's, London

18. *The Last Judgment*

Of course, Michaelangelo has Mary next to Christ in his depiction of The Last Judgment. Mary is always in Christ's presence.

Michaelangelo, *The Last Judgment*, altar wall, 1536–41, Vatican City, Rome

The Magnificence of Mary

Magnificence comes from two Latin words.

Magnum means great.

Facere means to make or do.

Magnificence means to make or do something great.

Mary is the embodiment
and definition of magnificence.

Mary's Yes changed the world
and continues to change us.

Many thanks to the following individuals
for their enthusiastic support of this book:

William Jens Jensen

Charles Wick

Roxanne and J. Bruce Murphy

John-Scott Legg

Bill Kelly

Stephan O'Reilly

Linda Solari Reilly